# Contents

# Introduction

## Why numeracy?

Developing a strong foundation in understanding numbers is essential for all children to move forward in their education and in their awareness of the world around them. As children become familiar with how numbers work, they are able to take a more active part in our world.

Numbers can be fun for children! Simple, enjoyable numeracy activities enable them to count competently and confidently; recognize shapes, patterns, and sequences; identify and write numerals; and equate them with quantities.

## Why in English?

Learning and playing with numbers in English, and developing numerical ability through English, is a good example of holistic learning. Having children work simultaneously through English and with numbers increases their understanding in both areas, establishing a strong foundation for their future learning. Exploring numerical and mathematical concepts within an English-speaking environment will also enhance children's experience of numeracy training in their own language, transferring skills and empowering children to become agents in their own learning.

## How to use the Numeracy Books

The Numeracy Books will add enrichment to early mathematics for all young learners. They can be used as a valuable numeracy supplement to any preschool English course, allowing you to work through the book at your own pace. In the books, you will find presentation, familiarization, and practice pages, consolidating and extending the children's understanding of number work.

Numeracy Book 2 provides a review of numbers 1–10, before children begin working carefully through numbers 11–20. The number work is supplemented with practice activities around mathematical concepts such as measuring, missing numbers, recognizing patterns and sequences, and *before* and *after*. When new numbers are presented, there are opportunities for practicing writing the numeral as well as recognizing the related quantity. Further activities practice equating the numerals to quantities by matching, counting, circling, coloring, and drawing. Activities that concentrate on breaking numbers between 10 and 20 into tens and units help to establish a strong foundation for later work on addition. Children develop listening skills by working with aural cues to identify numbers, continue patterns and sequences, write appropriate numerals, and draw appropriate quantities. In the final two activity pages (*I can …*), children are encouraged to summarize what they have learned and feel proud of their achievements.

# Activity types

## Trace. / Match. / Connect.

Encourage children to trace along the dashed lines from left to right, where appropriate, following the arrows. When they have to match or connect numerals to pictures, encourage them to stop and count first.

## Write.

In Level 2, children begin to move from tracing numerals to writing them freehand. If the children say the English words for the numbers aloud as they write them, they will quickly develop their productive knowledge of these numbers.

## Color. / Draw.

Young children will have varying levels of fine motor skills. Some will be able to color pictures very carefully, and some will color "over" a picture rather than color between the lines. Similarly, the children's ability to draw pictures freehand will be varied. It is more important that the children are engaging with and learning from the activity than coloring or drawing perfectly.

## Count. / Order.

It can be helpful for children to use their pen or pencil to mark the items as they count them, saying the number in English as they do so. When connecting or writing numbers in the correct order, encourage them to move their counting finger or pencil at the same time as they say the numbers aloud.

## Add.

In Level 2, children are gently introduced to the concept of working with numbers above 10 in tens and units, paving the way to future exploration of addition. In these activities, children combine tens and units to make numbers between ten and twenty.

## Listen.

For activities that require the children to listen for information, make sure they understand what they have to do before they listen. Demonstrate what they have to do and where. Then play the audio as many times as necessary. Where the children are required to recognize shape and color words in the audio, it may be necessary to review the English words for these before they listen.

## Measure.

These activities enable children to take their first steps in measuring. Children first learn to recognize the biggest item in a group. Body language can be used to demonstrate the meaning of "biggest" and transfer this concept to the activity on the page.

At this stage, specific units of measurement (e.g., centimeters) are not used; instead, children are taught the skill of looking from the item to the measuring scale and identifying the appropriate number.

# Number activities and games

## Numeral recognition and formation

Practice numeral formation away from the page, employing gross as well as fine motor skills; for example:

- Draw numbers on each other's backs.
- Draw numbers on the ground in chalk.
- Draw numbers in sand.
- Draw numbers in the air. Alternatively, the teacher or children can do this while other children watch and say what the number is.
- Ask the class to identify and say any numerals they can find in their classroom or environment, for example, on the walls, on computers, on book covers, on notices, on calendars, etc.

## Counting

Vary the counting style; for example:

- Count and clap, step, or stamp.
- Count and bang a drum or tap a desk gently.
- Count silently by moving lips and showing fingers.
- Count items around the school and adjacent areas.
- The teacher or one of the children claps, taps the desk, or bangs a drum. Children listen and say how many beats they heard.
- Say a number familiar to the children and ask them to count to that number.

When young children are counting items or pictures, encourage them to be slow and careful, as the speed at which they count aloud is often different from the speed at which they move their hands or fingers from item to item.

## Number order

Give opportunities for children to practice using numbers in the correct order; for example:

- Have children sit in a circle and say the numbers around the circle in order.
- Have children sit in a circle and roll a ball to each other, saying the next number each time the ball is rolled.
- Give number cards to different children and ask them to say their numbers in order.
- Give number cards to different children and have them arrange themselves in order.
- Count around the class with each child saying a number. When you say *Stop*, they stop. When you say *Go*, they start again but in the opposite direction around the class.

With confident classes, you can ask the children to do the activities using the numbers in reverse order.

## Quantities

Practice equating numbers with quantities; for example:

- Give a number and ask children to form groups of that number.
- Give a number and ask children to hold up, find, or bring you that number of items.
- Give a number and ask a child to clap, stamp, step, jump, or pat their head that number of times. The rest of the class watch and count aloud.
- Give a number and ask children to take that number of items (e.g., pencils) out of a bag without looking inside it.
- Arrange piles of items, e.g., fourteen books and seventeen books. Give a number and ask children to point to or stand next to the correct pile.

## How many?

Play counting games. Encourage the rest of the class to count as one child does an activity; for example:

- How many times can they bounce a balloon or throw and catch it?
- How many bubbles can they blow?
- How many items can they find; e.g., crayons in a tray, or chairs in a classroom?
- How many times can they hop / jump, etc.?
- Hold up a number card behind your back. Ask the children *How many?* The children call out their guesses. Show the children the number card. Repeat the game, inviting children to hide a number card for the rest of the class to guess.

**1** Trace, count, and match.

**2** Follow and write the numbers.

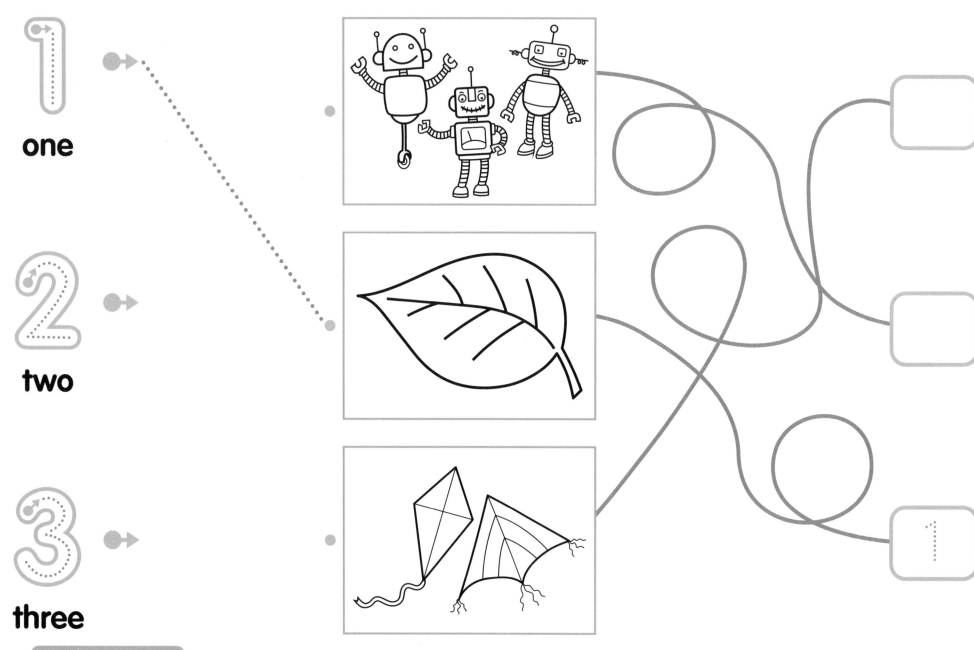

one

two

three

**1** Trace, count, and match.

**2** Follow and write the numbers.

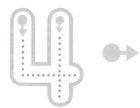

four

five

six

**1** Trace, count, and match.

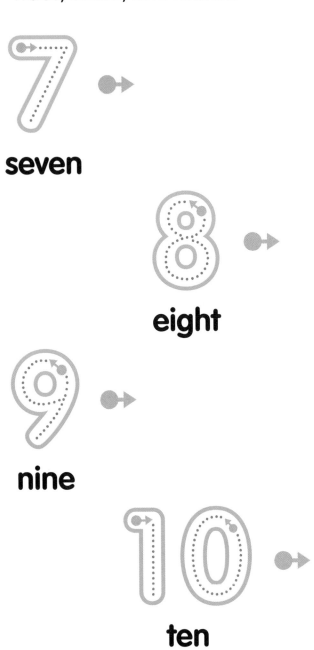

seven

eight

nine

ten

**2** Follow and write the numbers.

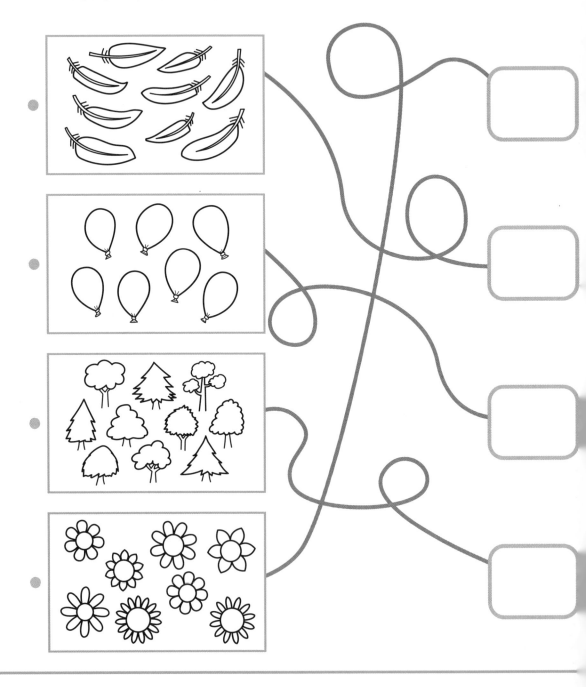

**1** Write the missing numbers.    **2** Trace.

| | | | | |
|---|---|---|---|---|
| **1** one | **2** two | three | **4** four | five |
| **6** six | seven | **8** eight | nine | ten |

**1** 🔊 001 Listen and follow. Write the numbers.   **2** 🔊 002 Listen again and check.

🔊003 Listen and color.    Count and write.

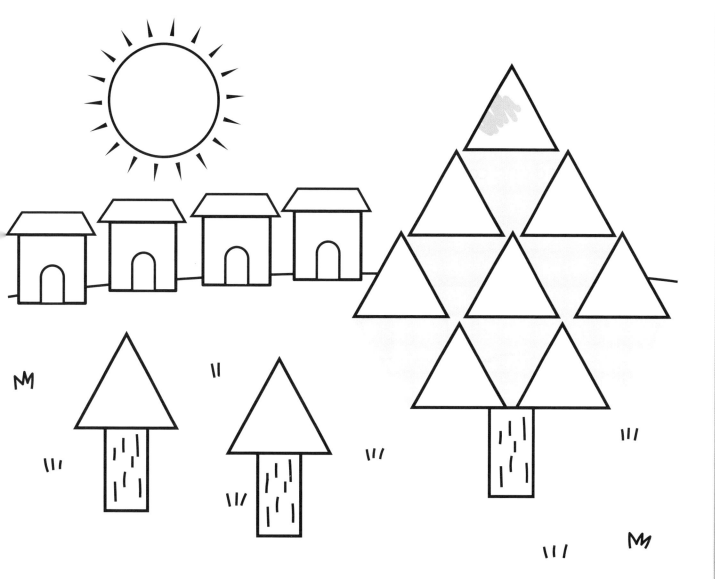

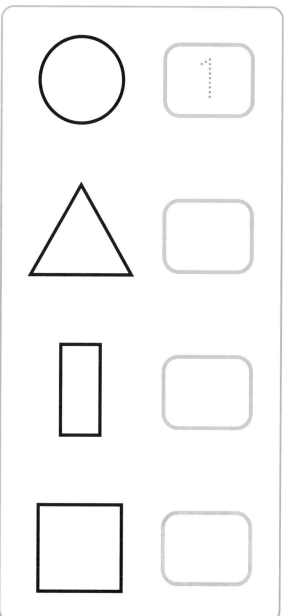

**1** Trace and write **number 11**.

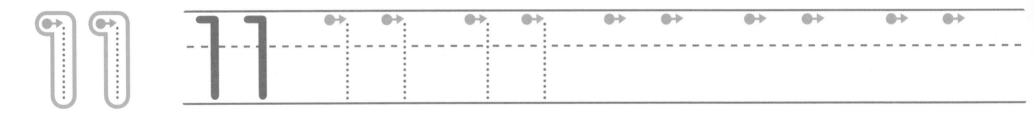

**2** Color the circles ◯ and count.

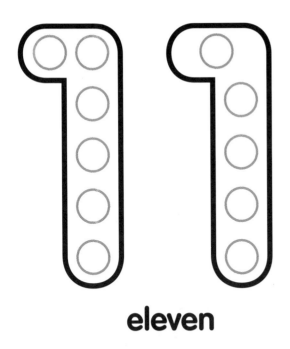

**eleven**

**3** Find and color **number 11**. Connect the number and word.

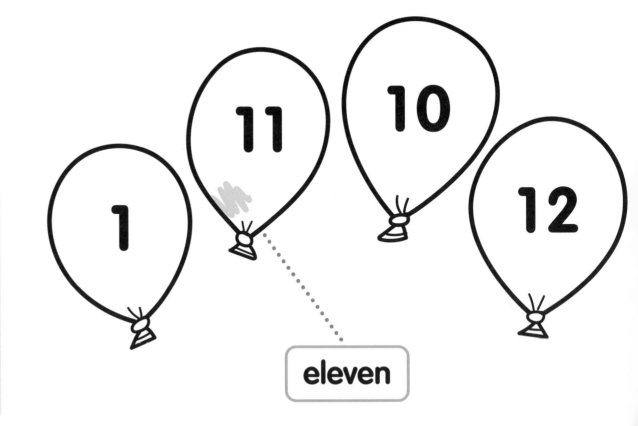

**eleven**

**1** Trace and write **number 12**.

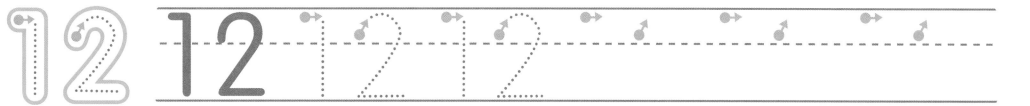

**2** Color the circles ⭕ and count.

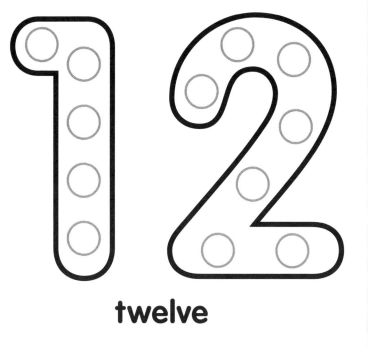

twelve

**3** Find and color **number 12**. Connect the number and word.

twelve

**1** 🔊004 Listen and color. **2** Count and match.

 → 

**eleven**

 →

**twelve**

**1** Count and write.

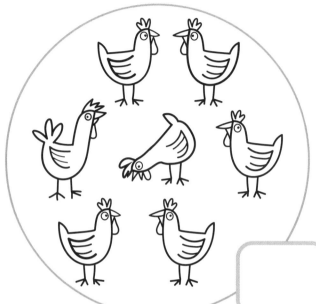

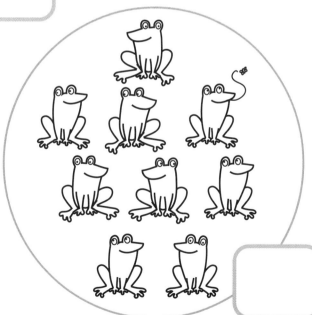

**1** Trace the numbers. Connect in order.

# 1 Look, count, and write.

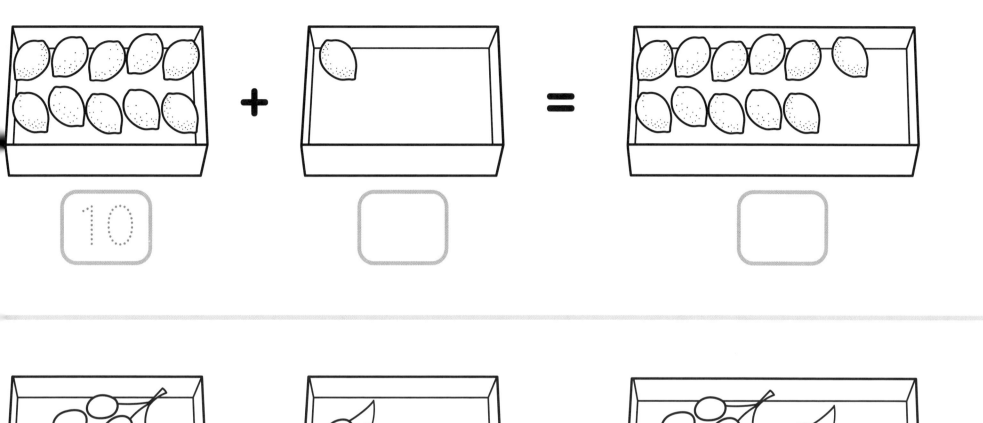

**1** Trace and write **number 13**.

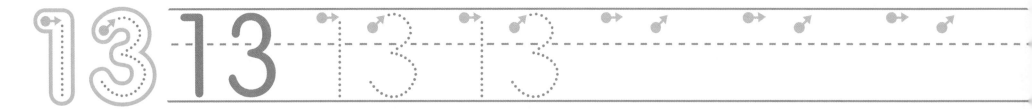

**2** Color the circles ◯ and count.

thirteen

**3** Find and color **number 13**. Connect the number and word.

10    13

12    3

thirteen

**1** Trace and write **number 14**.

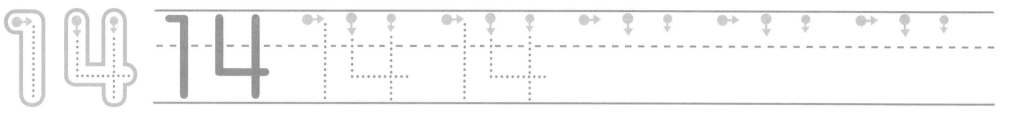

**2** Color the circles ◯ and count.

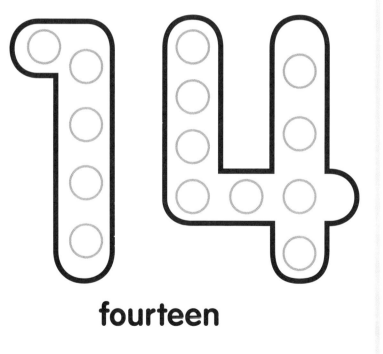

**fourteen**

**3** Find and color **number 14**. Connect the number and word.

14   13   11   4

fourteen

1 Color the circles ◯ yellow. Color the squares ☐ red.

2 Count and match. Color the number the same.

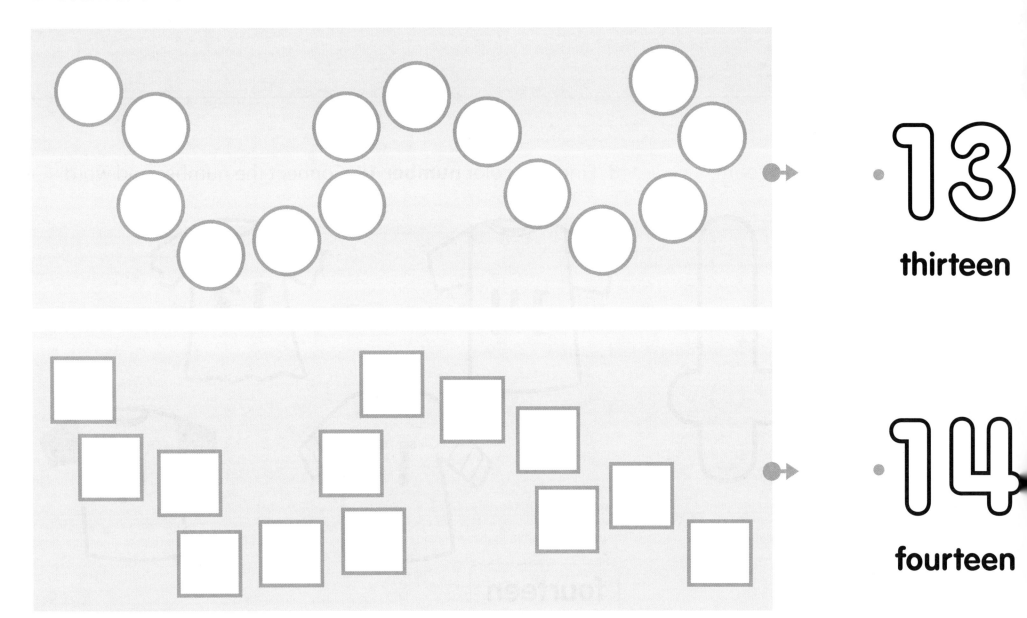

13 thirteen

14 fourteen

**1** Count and write.    **2** Connect the groups in order.

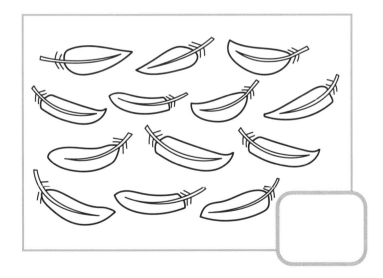

**1** 🔊 005 Listen and write.　**2** Draw.

**1** Count and write.  **2** Add, draw, and write.

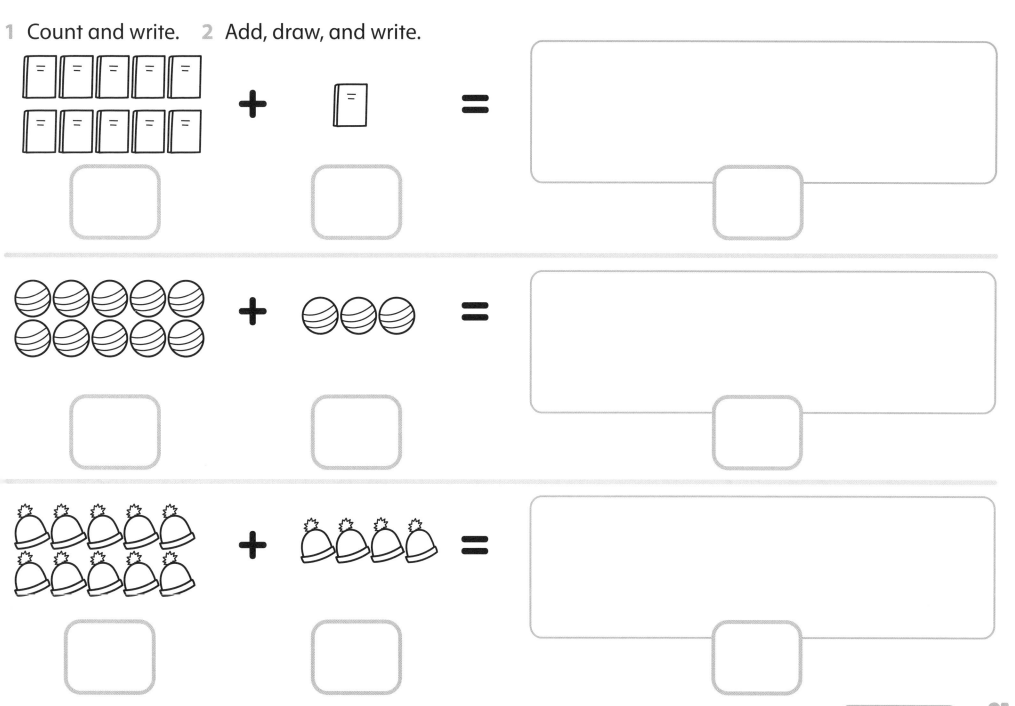

**1** Trace and write **number 15**.

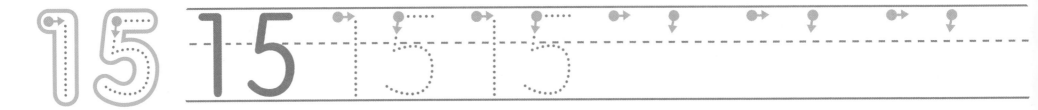

**2** Color the circles ◯ and count.

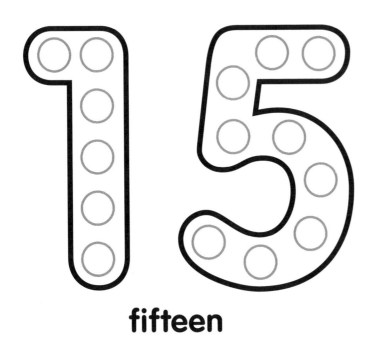

fifteen

**3** Find and color **number 15**. Connect the number and word.

5

11

15

1

fifteen

**1** Trace and write **number 16**.

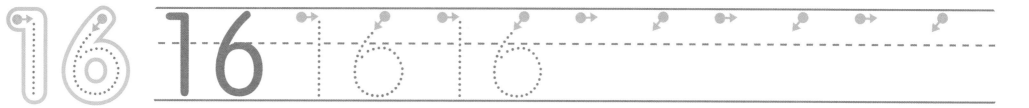

**2** Color the circles ◯ and count.

sixteen

**3** Find and color **number 16**. Connect the number and word.

1

6

15

16

sixteen

**1** 🔊 006 Listen and color.    **2** 🔊 007 Listen and draw.

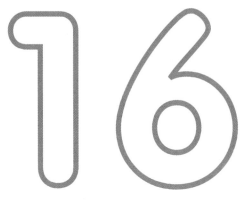

1 Draw a web. Connect and say in order.

16   9   10   1   8   2   15   7   3   11   6   4   5   14   13   12

**1** Count and mark the different fruits. Write.

**1** Count and write.

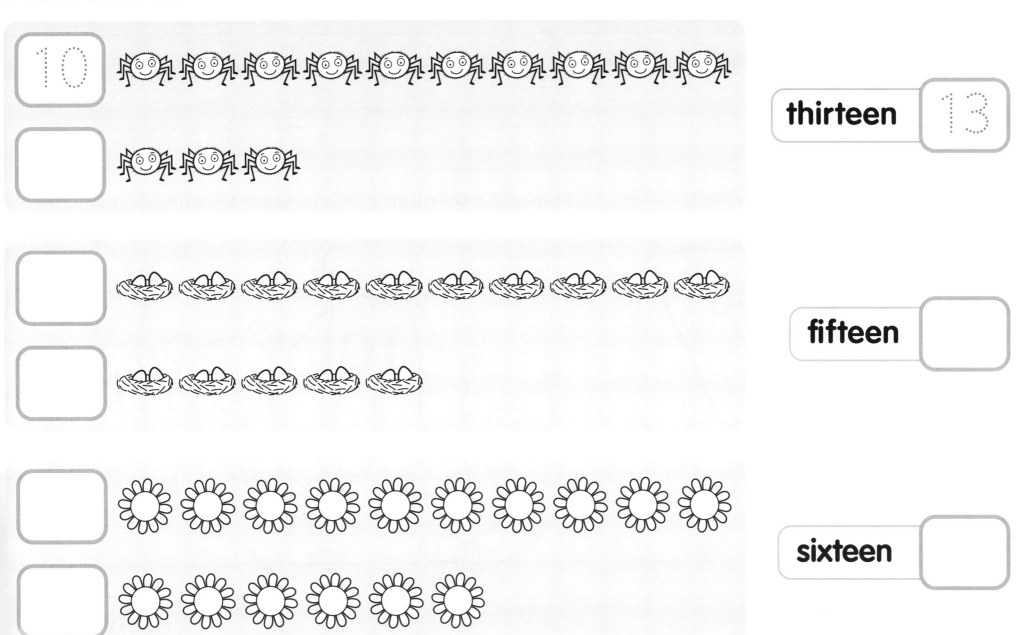

thirteen | 13

fifteen

sixteen

**1** Trace and write **number 17**.

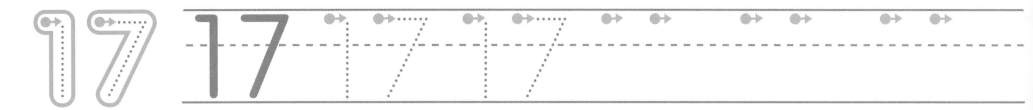

**2** Color the circles ◯ and count.

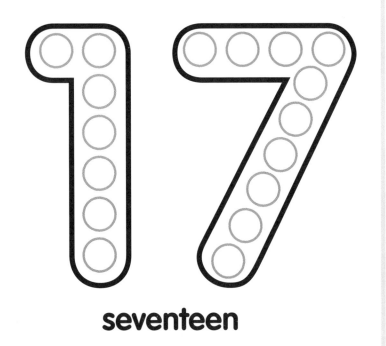

seventeen

**3** Find and color **number 17**. Connect the number and word.

seventeen

Trace and write **number 18**.

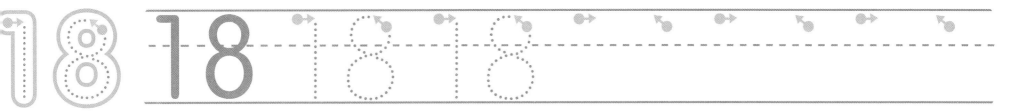

**2** Color the circles ◯ and count.

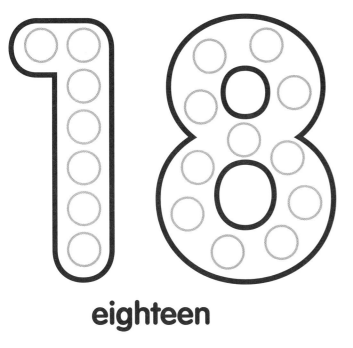

eighteen

**3** Find and color **number 18**. Connect the number and word.

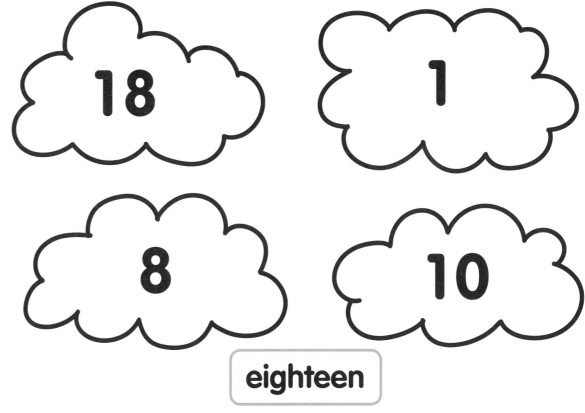

18

1

8

10

eighteen

**1** Find **17** and **18**. Color **17** green. Color **18** gray.

**2** How many things are green?  [ ]  How many things are gray?  [ ]

**1** 🔊008 Listen and color.

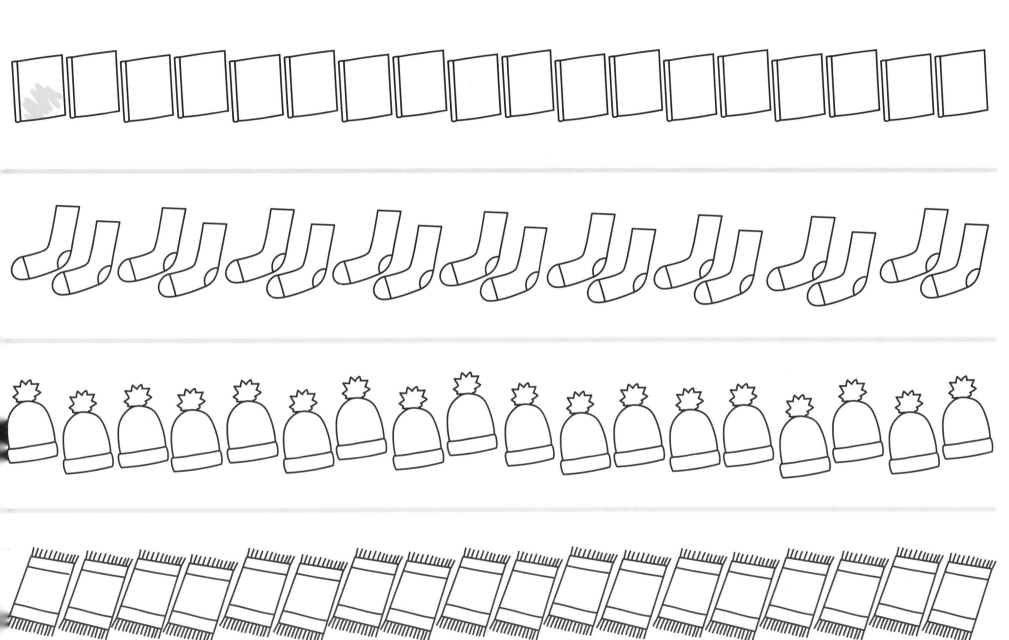

**1** Count and mark. Write.

1 Color the triangles △ green. Color the rectangles ▯ blue. Count and write.

2 Match and color the number the same.

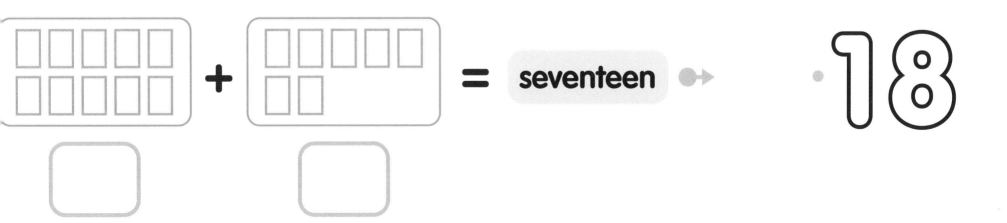

**1** Trace and write **number 19**.

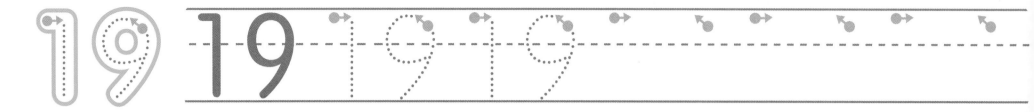

**2** Color the circles ◯ and count.

**nineteen**

**3** Find and color **number 19**. Connect the number and word.

11

19

9

16

nineteen

**1** Trace and write **number 20**.

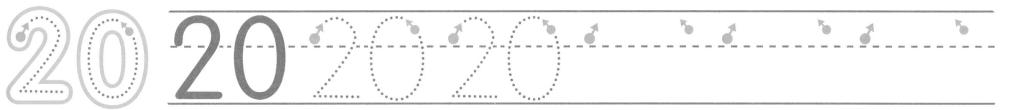

**2** Color the circles ◯ and count.

twenty

**3** Find and color **number 20**. Connect the number and word.

twenty

**1** Connect the stones ⬭ and write the numbers.    **2** Count and write. How many frogs 🐸?

1 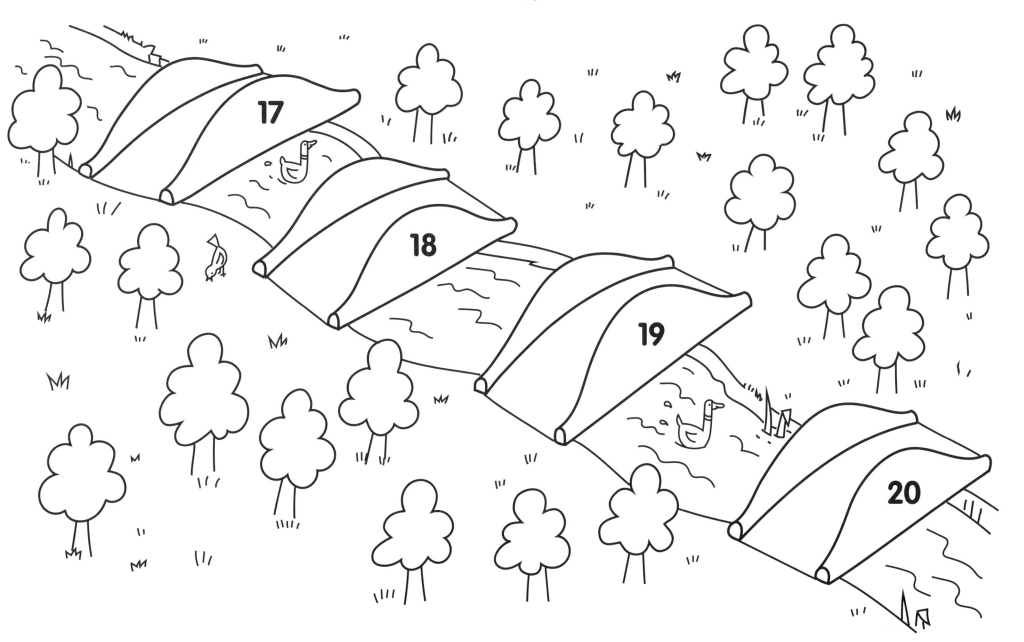 **009** Listen and color. 2 Count and color **20** trees 🌳.

**1** Count and write. Color.

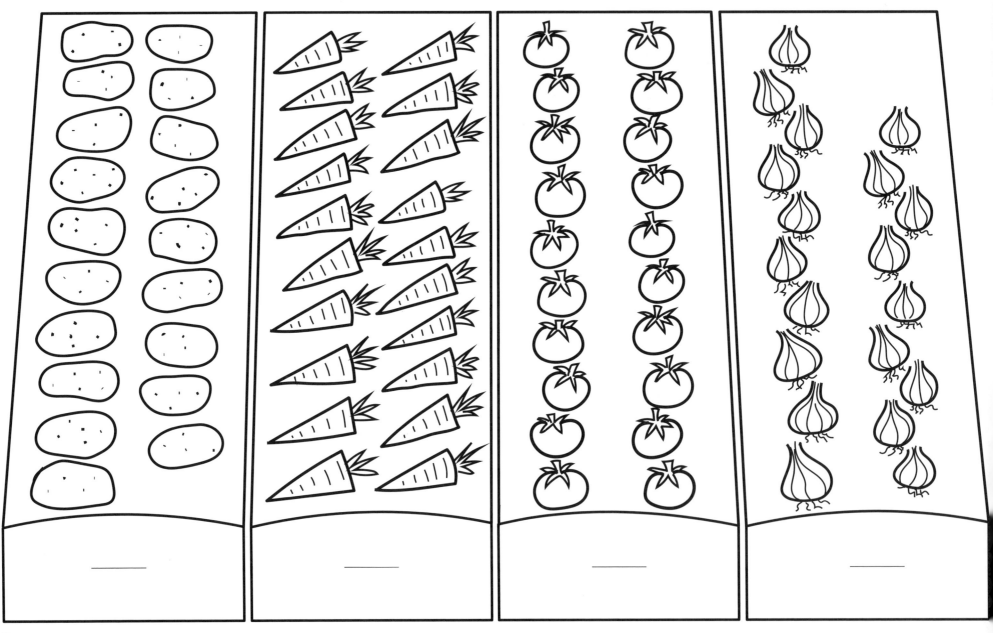

**1** Count and write.

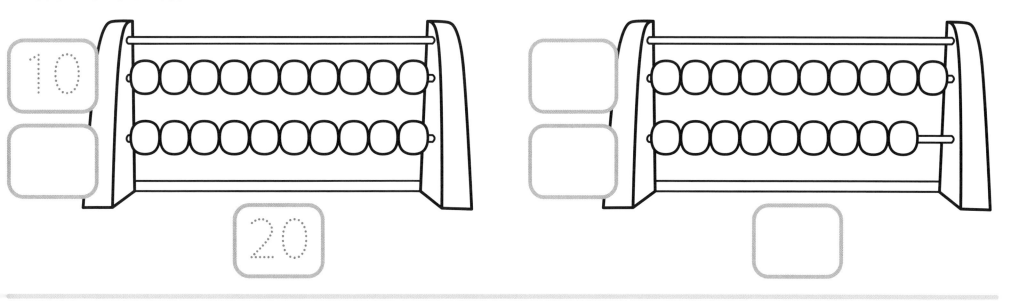

**2** Look at the numbers and draw.　　**3** Add and write.

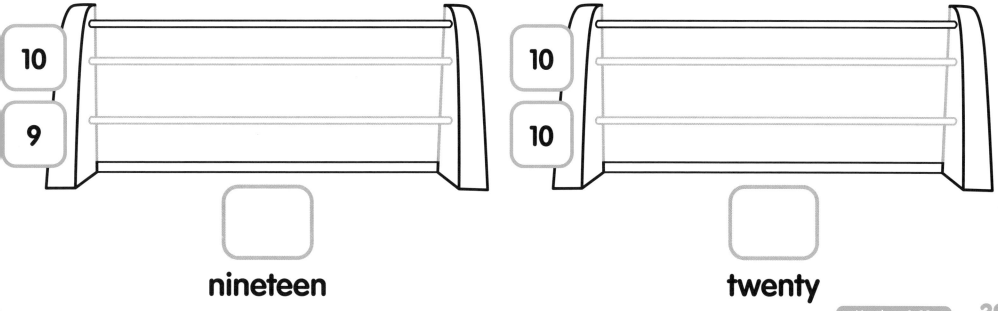

nineteen　　　　　　　　　　　twenty

**1** Circle and color the biggest.

**1** Look, measure, and write.

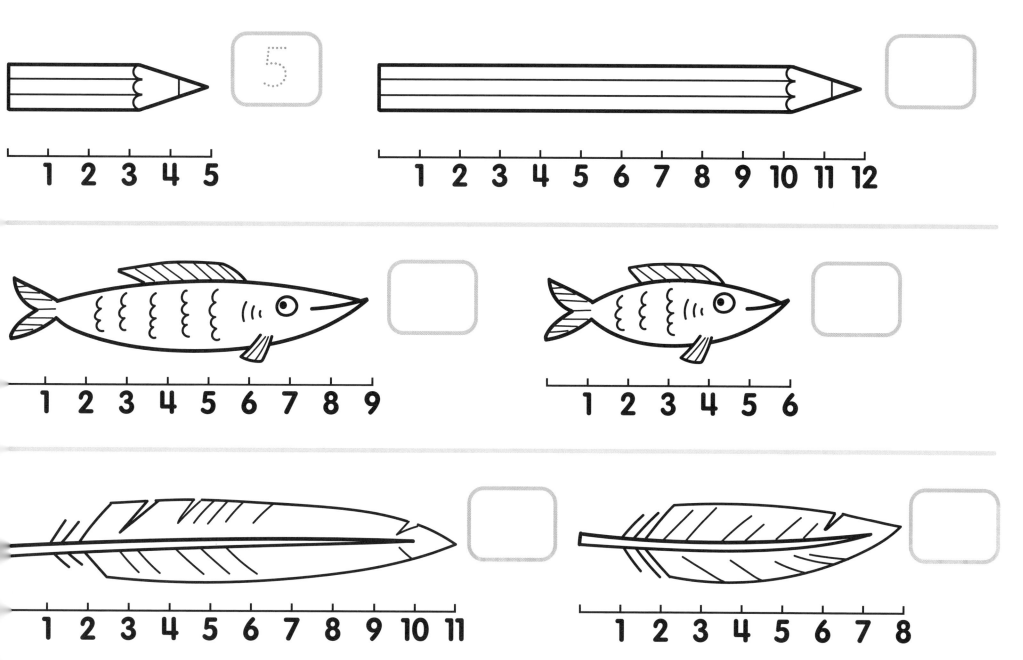

**1** Look, measure, and color. **2** Write.

Numbers 1–20 Review   Measuring

**1** Look, measure, and write.

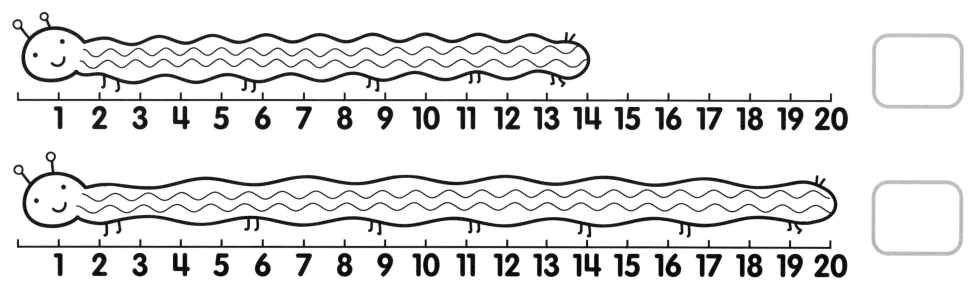

**2** Look at the numbers and complete.

11

19

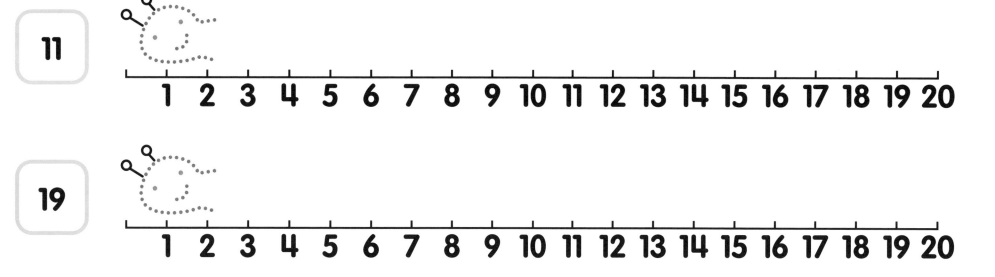

**1** What's different? Count and write.

**2** Draw more balloons 🎈, teddy bears 🧸, balls ⚽, and books 📕 to make the pictures the same.

**1** Write the missing numbers. Color.

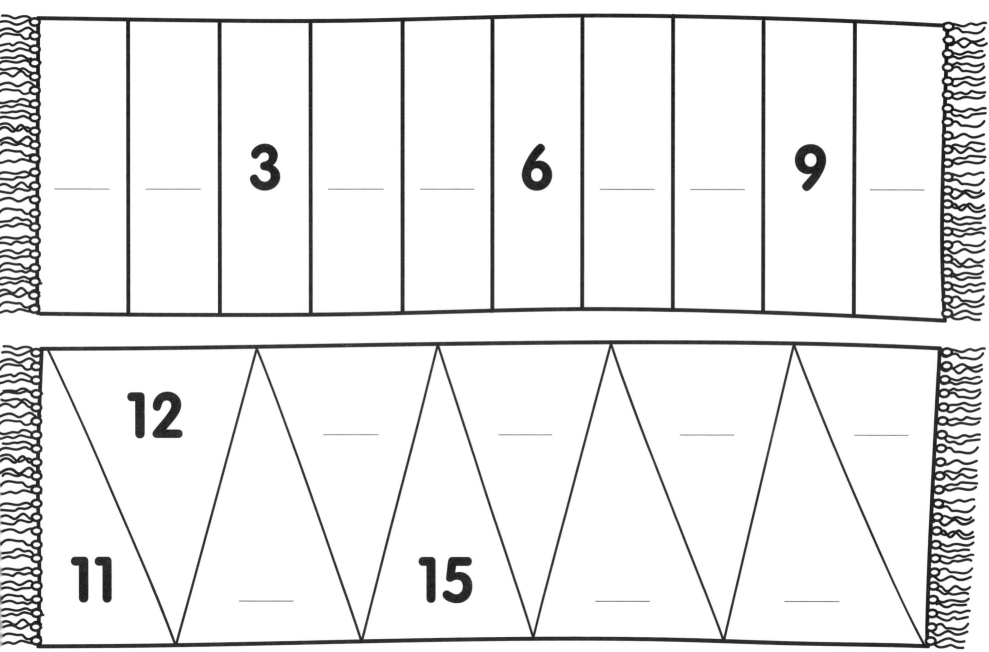

1 Look. What's next? Write the missing numbers.    2 🔊010 Listen and check.

**1** 🔊011 Listen and write.    **2** Draw.

**1** Number the balloons in order. **1** is the smallest and **5** is the biggest.　　**2** Connect in order.

Numbers 1–20 Review　　Compare before / after

**1** Look and number the pictures in order. Color.

1

**1** Color the number **before** 5 yellow. Color the number **after** 5 red.

1  2  3  4  5  6  7  8  9  10

**2** Draw a ☐ around the number **before** 19. Draw a ◯ around the number **after** 19.

11  12  13  14  15  16  17  18  19  20

**3** Draw a △ around the number **before** 11. Draw a ☐ around the number **after** 14.

1  2  3  4  5  6  7  8  9  10  11  12  13  14  15  16  17  18  19  20

# I can ...

**1** Trace the numbers and count.

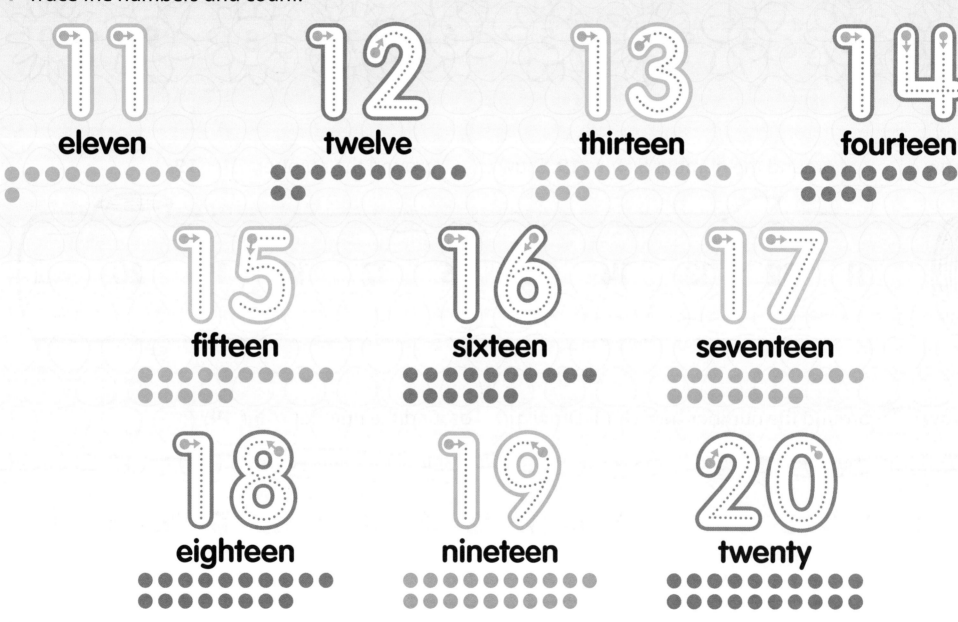

11 eleven

12 twelve

13 thirteen

14 fourteen

15 fifteen

16 sixteen

17 seventeen

18 eighteen

19 nineteen

20 twenty

**2** Do the activities and color the shapes.

Say the missing number.

11      12      13

14     16     17

18     19     20

Say the number **before** 19.

Say the number **after** 19.

Say what's next.

11   13   15   17

Count from **1** to **10**.

1, 2, … 10

Look, measure, and say.

1  2  3  4  5  6  7

Count from **11** to **20**.

11, 12, … 20

53

# Audio transcripts

## Page 8

🔊 001–002 **Listen and follow. Write the numbers. Listen again and check.**

1 cow, 2 cats, 3 horses, 4 chickens, 5 birds, 6 dogs, 7 donkeys, 8 frogs, 9 bees, 10 ducks

## Page 9

🔊 003 **Listen and color.**

Color the triangles green.
Color the circle yellow.
Color the rectangles brown.
Color the squares blue.

## Page 12

🔊 004 **Listen and color.**

Color number 11 red.
Color number 12 blue.

## Page 20

🔊 005 **Listen and write.**

I have 10 carrots.
I have 13 peas.
I have 14 tomatoes.

## Page 24

🔊 006 **Listen and color.**

Number 15 is green.
Number 16 is yellow.

## Page 24

🔊 007 **Listen and draw.**

Draw 15 circles.
Draw 16 triangles.

## Page 31

🔊 008 **Listen and color.**

Color 8 books.
Color 17 socks.
Color 11 hats.
Color 18 rugs.

## Page 37

🔊 009 **Listen and color.**

Color bridge 17 brown.
Color bridge 18 green.
Color bridge 19 red.
Color bridge 20 blue.

## Page 46

🔊 010 **Listen and check.**

Star: 15, 16, 15, 16, 15
Sun: 10, 12, 14, 16, 18
Moon: 19, 18, 17, 16, 15

## Page 47

🔊 011 **Listen and write.**

I have 11 eggs.
I have 12 potatoes.
I have 13 bananas.

## Page 49

🔊 012–013 **Listen and write. Listen again and check.**

Number 1: sheep, Number 2: frog, Number 3: horse, Number 4: duck, Number 5: cat, Number 6: chicken, Number 7: dog

# Answer key

**Page 4**
1 leaf, 2 kites, 3 robots

**Page 5**
4 monsters, 5 teddy bears, 6 umbrellas

**Page 6**
7 balloons, 8 flowers, 9 feathers, 10 trees

**Page 7**
3, 5, 7, 9, 10

**Page 8**
1 cow, 2 cats, 3 horses, 4 chickens, 5 birds,
6 dogs, 7 donkeys, 8 frogs, 9 bees, 10 ducks

**Page 9**
1 triangles – green, circle – yellow,
rectangles – brown, squares – blue
2 1 circle, 10 triangles, 3 rectangles,
4 squares

**Page 12**
1 11 – red, 12 – blue
2 11 carrots, 12 pineapples

**Page 13**
7 chickens, 11 bees, 9 frogs, 12 birds

**Page 14**
1, 2, 3, 4, 5, 6, 7, 8, 9, 10, 11, 12

**Page 15**
10 + 1 = 11 lemons
10 + 2 = 12 grapes

**Page 18**
14 yellow circles, 13 red squares

**Page 19**
11 trees, 12 flowers, 13 feathers, 14 logs

**Page 20**
10 carrots, 13 peas, 14 tomatoes

**Page 21**
10 + 1 = 11 books
10 + 3 = 13 balls
10 + 4 = 14 hats

**Page 24**
1 15 – green, 16 – yellow
2 15 circles, 16 triangles

**Page 25**
1, 2, 3, 4, 5, 6, 7, 8, 9, 10, 11, 12, 13, 14, 15, 16

**Page 26**
6 bananas, 15 apples, 16 grapes, 5 lemons

**Page 27**
10 (spiders), 3 (spiders), 13 ( spiders)
10 (nests), 5 (nests), 15 (nests)
10 (flowers), 6 (flowers), 16 (flowers)

**Page 30**
5 are green, 4 are gray

**Page 31**
8 books, 17 socks, 11 hats, 18 rugs

**Page 32**
8 apples, 18 flowers, 17 bees, 7 spiders

**Page 33**
10 + 8 = 18
10 + 7 = 17

**Page 36**
1 1, 2, 3, 4, 5, 6, 7, 8, 9, 10, 11, 12, 13, 14,
15, 16, 17, 18, 19, 20
2 9 frogs

**Page 37**
Bridge 17 is brown.
Bridge 18 is green.
Bridge 19 is red.
Bridge 20 is blue.

**Page 38**
19 potatoes, 20 carrots, 20 tomatoes,
19 onions

**Page 39**
1 10 + 10 = 20
   10 + 9 = 19
   10 + 9 = 19
   10 + 10 = 20
3 19, 20

**Page 40**
Children circle and color the biggest cat,
sheep, chicken, and mouse.

**Page 41**
pencils – 5, 12
fish – 9, 6
feathers – 11, 8

**Page 42**
11, 7, 14

**Page 43**
14, 20

**Page 44**
Picture A – 8 balloons, 3 teddy bears,
6 balls, 7 books
Picture B – 4 balloons, 2 teddy bears,
3 balls, 4 books

**Page 45**
The missing numbers are 1, 2, 4, 5, 7, 8, 10;
13, 14, 16, 17, 18, 19, 20

**Page 46**
15, 16, 15, 16, 15
10, 12, 14, 16, 18
19, 18, 17, 16, 15

**Page 47**
11 eggs, 12 potatoes, 13 bananas

**Page 48**
Children number the balloons 1 to 5 from
smallest to biggest and connect them
in order.

**Page 49**
sheep 1, frog 2, horse 3, duck 4, cat 5,
chicken 6, dog 7

**Page 50**
Top row – 5, 2
Middle row – 1
Bottom row – 3, 4

**Page 51**
1 4 is yellow, 6 is red
2 rectangle around 18, circle around 20
3 triangle around 10, square around 15

**Page 53**
Say the missing number – 15
Say the number before 19 – 18
Say the number after 19 – 20
Say what's next – 19
Look, measure, and say – 6
Count from 1 to 10 – 1, 2, 3, 4, 5, 6, 7, 8, 9, 10
Count from 11 to 20 – 11, 12, 13, 14, 15, 16,
17, 18, 19, 20

Great Clarendon Street, Oxford, OX2 6DP, United Kingdom

Oxford University Press is a department of the University of Oxford.
It furthers the University's objective of excellence in research, scholarship,
and education by publishing worldwide. Oxford is a registered trade
mark of Oxford University Press in the UK and in certain other countries

ISBN: 978 0 19 486288 2          Little Blue Dot 2 Numeracy Book

Printed in China

This book is printed on paper from certified and well-managed sources

ACKNOWLEDGEMENTS

*Illustrations by*: Judy Brown.

*The publisher would like to thank the following for permission to reproduce
cover photographs*: Shutterstock (artjazz, Avesun, cz, Kitsana1980, piyaphon,
Vandathai).